Welcome to 'Calm and Color.' This coloring book is designed to help you find peace and relaxation through the simple act of coloring. Each page is filled with intricate designs and positive affirmations to help you unwind and focus. Enjoy the journey to calmness.

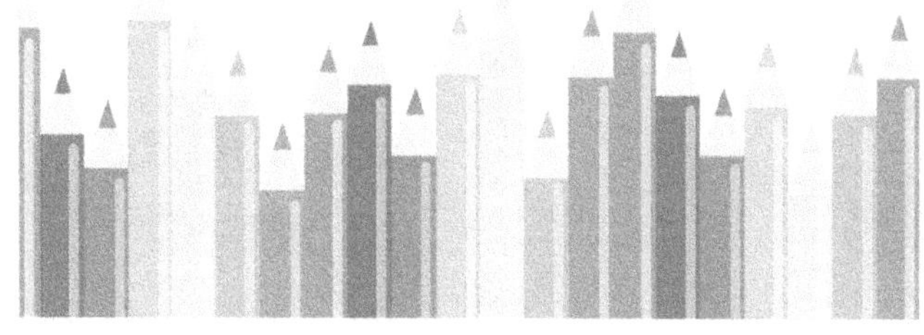

Find a quiet, comfortable space. Take a few deep breaths before you begin. Choose the page that speaks to you and start coloring. Focus on the patterns and let your mind relax.

Breathe deeply, you are in control.

As you colour, focus on your breath and let go of any tension you may be holding.

You are capable and strong.

Think of a place where you feel at peace and imagine yourself there."

One step at a time, one breath at a Time.

Notice the colors you choose. How do they make you feel?"

You are enough just as you are.

Focus on the details. Let your mind wander freely.

Embrace the present moment.

Let go of any thoughts of the past
or future. Be here now.

Peace begins with a single thought.

Notice the colors you choose. How
do they make you feel?

You are enough just as you are.

Focus on the details. Let your
mind wander freely.

Embrace the present moment.

Let go of any thoughts of the past or future. Be here now.

Inhale calm, exhale tension.

Think of something you are grateful for.

You are worthy of love and
happiness.

Focus on the sensation of the pen or pencil moving across the paper.

Trust in the process.

Notice your breathing as you colour.

You are a source of light and positivity."

Notice how you feel before, during, and after coloring.

You are calm, you are safe.

As you colour, repeat a calming mantra in your mind.

Every breath you take fills you
with calmness.

Take a moment to appreciate your creativity.

You are in the right place at the right time.

Feel the relaxation flowing through you as you color.

You are resilient and strong.

Imagine the colours bringing peace and calm to your body."

Every breath you take fills you
with calmness.

Take a moment to appreciate your creativity.

You are in the right place at the right time.

Feel the relaxation flowing through you
as you colour.

Thank you for taking the time to care for yourself through this coloring book. We hope you feel more relaxed and at peace. Take a moment to reflect on how you feel and any changes you've noticed. Remember, this book is always here for you whenever you need a moment of calm.

www.ingramcontent.com/pod-product-compliance
Lightning Source LLC
Chambersburg PA
CBHW072342270726
48659CB00023B/2310